Beachbum Berry's GROG LOG

A selection of vintage tropical drink recipes. Original creations, and new interpretations of old classics.

By Jeff Berry and Annene Kaye

AUTHORS' ACKNOWLEDGMENTS

Mahalo to Sven Kirsten, the Big Kahuna of urban archeologists, for sharing his knowledge and his archives and his artistry; to High Chief Otto von Stroheim, whose *mana* made this happen; to Stephen R. Remsberg, Tony Ramos, Ted Haigh, Kevin Kearns, Domenic Priore, John English, and Bob and Leroy of Oceanic Arts for their tips; to Michael Tsao of the Kahiki for his hospitality; to Dug Miller and Chester and Cheryl Crill for their generous contribution of vintage graphics; and to Bosko Hrnjak, Craig Pape, and Dan Vado, for putting the whole thing together so *wiki wiki.*

Written By
Jeff Berry & Annene Kaye

Editing, Art Direction & Layout By
Craig Pape

Additional Graphics By
Otto von Stroheim
Bosko Hrnjak

Published By
Dan Vado

Published by SLG Publishing 44 Race Street San Jose, CA 95126
Revised SLG Publishing Edition 2022
www.slgpubs.com
www.arkivatropika.com

INTRODUCTION

They're too sweet. They're too syrupy. They're even worse than the food. That's what your average Joe has to say about cocktails in Polynesian restaurants. But you can hardly blame Joe. The heyday of the tiki bar was two generations ago, and the know-how required to mix a good tropical drink vanished with them in the '70s, when the South Seas craze went south and popular tastes turned from Mai Tais to Margaritas. But when an "exotic" is made properly – when it achieves that perfect balance between sweet and sour, strong and light, fruity and dry – few pleasures can match it.

What makes a tropical drink something to savor, something to revisit, something to include in this volume? First, a truly great tropical has a beginning, a middle and an end: the heady initial sip, the fuller impact on the whole of the tongue, and the satisfying finish. A great tropical also stands up to its ice content, changing flavor but remaining palatable down to its last diluted drop. And it is always pleasing to the eye and the nose – especially the nose: The aromatic imprint of a multi-layered combination of ingredients, accented by the correct garnish, goes a long way toward making life worth living.

Hence this book. The time has come to restore the tropical drink to its former glory, especially in this era of technological burnout and cultural malaise: If we're going to feel like zombies, we may as well be drinking them.

PARADISE LOST ... AND FOUND

Mixing a good tropical drink is less a lost art than a complicated and costly one. Most bartenders simply don't have the time it takes to mix a proper exotic, and most bar owners don't want to pay for the proper ingredients. Order a Planter's Punch in even the swankiest watering hole and you're likely to get spiked Kool Aid.

It was not always so. Master mid-century restauranteurs Don the Beachcomber, Trader Vic, and the competition they spawned created some of the most spectacularly flavorful cocktails in American culinary history. From the 1930s right into the '70s – an unprecedented lifespan for a drink fad – Americans flocked to Polynesian restaurants, and not for the food. In 1960, the menu of the Islander in Beverly Hills offered "Pork Tiki," "Crab Puffs Rarotonga," "Polynesian Sacred Beef" and "Tonga Tabu Native Drum Steak," fresh "From the ovens of the ancient goddess of Bora Bora, Pele, Mistress of Flame." As you've no doubt guessed by now, the big draw was the bar. A place lived or died on the reputation of its exotic drinks, and the bartenders who knew them were valued employees. Since their recipes were their stock in trade, they revealed their secrets to no one.

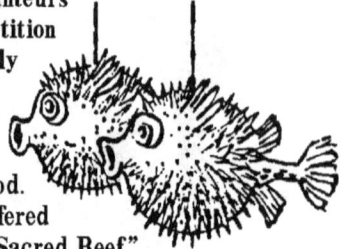

Over the years, a mystique grew around these alchemists who turned rum into gold. They wrote nothing down; if a competitor wanted your bistro's bar recipes, the only way to get them was to hire away your mixologist. But even that didn't work against counter-espionage tactics like those of Don the Beachcomber, who could have taught Oliver North a thing or two. "Infinite pains are taken," relates a 1948 *Saturday Evening Post* article, "to see to it that the service-bar help cannot memorize Don's various occult ingredients and proportions. Bottles are label-less; they bear numbers and letters instead. The recipes are in code and the mixers follow a pattern of code symbols indicating premixed ingredients, rather than actual names of fruit concentrates or rum brands. In this way, even if a rival restauranteur makes a raid on the Beachcomber help ... the renegade cannot take Don's recipes with him."

When Don the Beachcomber died, many of his recipes died with him. To this day, nobody really seems to know what went into his most famous creation, the Zombie. But another legendary mixologist broke Tabu in his old age; partly to help sell his own retail line of rums, drink mixes, salad dressings and condiments, Trader Vic published several cookbooks before he cashed in his taro chips.

The Trader's books reveal everything that went into *his* greatest creations – the Mai Tai, the Scorpion and the Fog Cutter, to name but a few. And toward the end of the Polynesian Pop era, other restauranteurs squeezed a few last bucks out of the fading fad by putting out cookbooks of their own, sometimes revealing one or two of the closely guarded secrets of their mixologists.

But all of these books have been unavailable for decades, while most of the best recipes were never *in* print to begin with. Consequently, today's bar guides can only tell you how to make pale – and sweet and syrupy – imitations of the originals.

To fill that void, we have combed through scores of old cookbooks, magazine articles, and bar menus; picked the brains of bartenders and barflies who were there; and criss-crossed the USA to field-test the potions of the few remaining Polynesian palaces. In the course of our research, we gained enough Dutch courage to invent some recipes of our own, and to re-interpret some vintage recipes that were almost, but not quite, worthy of re-printing (believe it or not, some tropical drinks really *were* too sweet and syrupy!). We've included these original and revised vintage recipes in the following pages. If the hardcore Polynesiacs among you don't recognize some of the names, that's because we followed the time-honored tiki bar tradition of changing the moniker if we changed the recipe. For the academically inclined, the original name and place of origin can be found at the bottom of each page.

One final caveat: This collection is by no means exhaustive. Or objective. As Theodore Sturgeon once said, "95 percent of everything is shit." Rather than a complete compendium of tropical drinks, these recipes are merely what we believe to be that other five percent; out of hundreds sampled, 84 drinks made the final cut.

Of course, no two people have exactly the same taste. So feel free to alter these recipes to suit yours. But before we knock back a few, let's head back a few years.

RUM AND TRUE RELIGION: A HISTORY OF TIKI TIPPLING

Where did the tropical drink come from? The original exotic cocktail was, fittingly enough, invented by the Pacific Islanders.

Order a Kava Bowl at Trader Vic's and you get a frothy concoction of rum and fruit juices. Order one on Vanuatu and you get a sticky porridge of chewed-up plant roots and human saliva. But before you send it back, consider that the roots are from the *Piper methysticum*, or kava plant, a powerful narcotic that makes the world go around in that part of the world.

Although now largely confined to the Melanesian island chain, kava drinking was practiced throughout the South Seas before European contact. Elaborate social rituals attended its consumption, which was performed with a religious zeal that puts our Happy Hour to shame. The islands of Tonga, Samoa, Hawaii and Papua New Guinea each have their own version of a kava origin myth: "The broad leaf that extinguishes chiefs" has sprouted variously from a vagina, the skin of a foot, or the hair of an armpit.

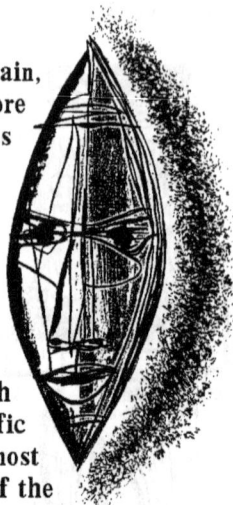

Preparation of the communal kava bowl hasn't changed much since 1773, when a naturalist on Captain Cook's second Pacific voyage observed Tahitian youths making a batch "in the most disgustful manner that can be imagined," chewing pieces of the root, spitting the macerated mass into a bowl, and mixing it with coconut milk, whereupon "they swallow this nauseous stuff as fast as possible."

This sight wasn't the only thing making British soldiers sick in the eighteenth century. It had been the tradition since 1655 to grant all seamen a daily half-pint ration of rum, which few of them were inclined to nurse. Gulping his "kill-divil" in one manly draught, Jack Tar found himself sailing three sheets to the wind whether there was any wind or not. If the Royal Navy tried to end this tradition, they'd have caused a mutiny that made the Bounty's look like a Princess Cruise. So in 1740 they did the next best thing: Admiral Edward Vernon, nicknamed "Old Grog" because of the grogram cloak he always wore, ordered the rum ration mixed with a quart of water. In 1795, over forty years after Scottish naval surgeon James Lind proved that citrus fruit prevented scurvy, lime juice was finally added to the mix. Thus was born the world's second tropical drink: The Navy Grog, named after Old Grog himself.

In the British West Indies, plantation owners added sugar to their rum, water and lime ... creating the Planter's Punch. The original recipe has been passed down for over 200 years as a bit of Jamaican doggerel: "One of sour, two of sweet, three of strong, four of weak."

4

Up in North America, the Colonists were also experimenting with rum. Early drinks included the Coow-woow (rum, water, ginger) and the Bombo (rum, water, sugar cane stick), but such primitive efforts pale before another early American recipe called the Byrd: "Fry six rashers of fat bacon; add one pint rum; eat the bacon and drink the syrup." The Byrd is named after Colonel William Byrd II, who recorded this cocktail in his journal of 1728; we doubt he drank too many of them, because he lived to see 1729.

Despite these and other decidedly non-tropical drinks (the Bellows-top Flip, very popular during the Revolution, called for sugar, cream, eggs, bitter beer and a gill of rum, beaten to a froth with a hot poker), Americans went on to make the rum cocktail their own over the next two centuries. Prominent among them was Jennings Cox, an engineer working a copper mine near the Cuban hamlet of Daiquiri – which is what he named the drink he invented there in 1896.

A few short years later, American soldiers fighting the Spanish American War in Cuba hit on the notion of mixing local rum with a new American beverage called Coca Cola; with a squeeze of lime, the mixture became the Cuba Libre, which teenagers everywhere have since come to know and love and puke as "Rum and Coke."

But the greatest innovator of the rum drink was neither a copper miner nor a foot soldier. He was a bootlegger. At least, that was the rumor in 1934, when the dapper Texan opened a tiny 25 seat bar near the corner of Hollywood Boulevard and McCadden Place. Nobody knew much about the real Ernest Raymond Beaumont-Gantt, and that's just the way he liked it. So much so, in fact, that he had his name legally changed ... to Donn Beach, short for Don the Beachcomber.

Donn was good with names, and good with drinks, and good with drink names. Word quickly got around about his "rum rhapsodies," innovative concoctions like the Vicious Virgin, the Missionary's Downfall, the Cobra's Fang and the Shark's Tooth. But it was the Zombie that really put Donn on the map. Legend has it that he whipped it up one day to help a hung-over customer get through an important business meeting. When Donn later asked how the cure worked, the customer said, "I felt like the living dead – it made a zombie out of me."

5

In no time at all, Donn was the toast of the Hollywood film crowd, and in 1937 he built a Polynesian Palace for them to spend their money in. Don the Beachcomber's became the template for hundreds of South Seas-themed restaurants over the next forty years, a style urban archeologist Sven Kirsten has dubbed Polynesian Pop. "Like an island in the urban sea," writes Kirsten in his *Book of Tiki* , "the Polynesian paradise was designed to be a refuge from the Metropolis that surrounded it. Upon entering, all the senses were assailed: Bamboo, rattan, tapa cloth and imported woods provided the basic texture. Tropical plants and palm trees with exotic birds in concealed cages served as flora and fauna, while lava rock waterfalls and their connecting streams babbled under bridges that led to rooms with strange names like Bora Bora Lounge and Cannibal Hut, where a 'tropical rainstorm' effect might shower on the corrugated tin roofing and run off down the glass partitions. Water was complemented by the original element, fire ... burning in torches and miniature volcanos, throwing a flickering light on black-velvet paintings of nude beauties. An array of found objects from all over the world dangled from the ceiling: fish traps, crates, coconuts, weapons, puffer fish and Japanese fishnet floats, most of them turned into dim lanterns, seemed to tell tales of faraway lands."

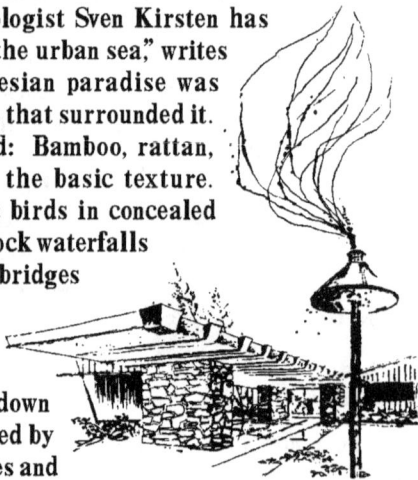

This turned out to be just what America wanted. Not just in 1937, but for the next forty years. In the '30s, when most Americans couldn't afford world travel, these exotic trappings were the closest many would ever get to the fabled mysteries of the Orient. In the '40s, when thousands of American G.I.s *did* go there, and wished they hadn't, the fad nevertheless grew even more popular when the South Seas were romanticized anew by James Michener's *Tales of the South Pacific* . In the '50s, the Eisenhower-era's stifling middle class conformity and repressive, paranoid morality made the lure of the Primitive even more strongly felt: In the dark, mysterious, pagan womb of the tiki bar, Organization Man could escape the spectre of the A-bomb and the 30-year mortgage.

The Island theme got another shot in the arm when Hawaii was granted Statehood in 1959; by the '60s, there were more tikis in suburban America than in the entire South Pacific. Not only were there hundreds of tiki bars, but also tiki apartment buildings ("Aloha Arms"), trailer parks ("Kona Kai Mobile Village"), fast food drive-throughs ("Luau Chicken"), bowling alleys ("Samoa Lanes"), fashion outlets ("Boutiki"), entertainment centers ("Holo Wai Miniature

Golf"), and even whole theme parks (the 12 acre "Tiki Gardens," featuring a "Polynesian Adventure Trail, eight fascinating shops, Trader Frank's Restaurant" ... and exotic creatures like Chang the peacock).

Donn Beach surfed this tidal wave until it crashed on the rocky shores of the emerging Counterculture; somehow, sipping a Coolie Cup just didn't seem like the best way to unwind after a Vietnam War protest rally. But before the end came, Don the Beachcomber's had mushroomed into a nationwide chain of 16 restaurants.

And his chief competitor had morphed from a hash-slinger in an Oakland rib joint called Hinky Dink's ... into Trader Vic, the High Chief of an even bigger empire that at its height boasted over 20 restaurants around the world, from the flagship in San Francisco to such ports o' call as London, Hamburg, Bangkok and Beirut.

Victor Bergeron freely admitted ripping off Donn's idea; a 1938 visit to the Beachcomber's thriving concern convinced him to go native as well, whereupon Hinky Dink's became "Vic's Trading Post." Although Vic had never been to the Islands, he assumed the identity of a salty South Seas roustabout. Ever the showman, he regaled his patrons with tales of how he had lost a leg on the high seas – then invited them to stick their forks in his wooden one.

In reality, he had been fitted for his artificial leg after contracting tuberculosis as a child. But reality was exactly what Polynesian restaurants *weren't* selling, a fact the Trader knew all too well. He even had to go to court to defend his version of how he came up with the Mai Tai, an invention other mixologists claimed for themselves. Vic won his case with this rather serendipitous tale: "I was behind my bar one day in 1944 talking with my bartender, and I told him that I was going to make the finest rum drink in the world. Just then Ham and Carrie Guild, some old friends from Tahiti, came in. Carrie tasted it, raised her glass, and said, 'Mai Tai – Roa Ae,' which in Tahitian means 'Out of this world – the best!' That's the name of the drink, I said, and we named it Mai Tai."

Although Trader Vic died in 1984, many of his restaurants are still open today. But if you don't happen to live near Beverly Hills, Emeryville, Chicago, Atlanta, Tokyo, Dusseldorf or Abu Dhabi, the best way to sample Vic's wares might very well be to mix them yourself.

GETTING STARTED

You'll need an ICE CRUSHER, a heavy duty BLENDER, and a metal COCKTAIL SHAKER with strainer top. Pick up a JUICE REAMER, a standard EIGHT OUNCE MEASURING CUP, and a set of kitchen MEASURING SPOONS at any supermarket or drug store, but make sure the spoons go down to 1/8 teaspoon. You'll find an EYE-DROPPER at just about any pharmacy.

Less easy to find is a SMALL MEASURING CUP with 1/4 ounce increments, sometimes called a "pharmacist's jigger." The closest you might be able to come is a liquor store item called a SHOT GLASS POURER, a shot glass with 1/2 ounce, 3/4 ounce, one ounce, and 1 1/2 ounce markings. If all else fails, you can always buy a JIGGER, a double-sided metal pouring cup that holds 3/4 ounce on one side and 1 1/2 ounces (one jigger) on the other. (For more on pouring, see "Measuring" on page 13.)

Last but not least, no tiki bar can do without the proper GLASSWARE: small and large cocktail glasses, V-shaped Pilsener glasses, tall Collins glasses, oversized brandy snifters, wide-mouthed double old-fashioned glasses ... and, of course, your personal collection of TIKI MUGS AND BOWLS.

Most Polynesian restaurants either sold tiki mugs in their gift shops, or gave them away free when you ordered their signature drink, or had them pilfered by souvenir-hungry diners. Consequently, today you can find a wide array of mugs at swap meets, thrift stores and antique malls. (Or you can buy them new: See our RESOURCE GUIDE on the last page of this book.)

BARTENDING ON A BUDGET

So now you've got the hardware and the glassware, and you've already blown your budget. If so, may we make a few suggestions before you pawn your watch to buy your booze?

First, thumb through the recipes and pick out a simple drink that interests you, one with only a few ingredients. Purchase only those ingredients; then, as you try other recipes, buy the new necessary ingredients as you need them. Over time, you'll have amassed a fully stocked bar without feeling the sting of one large, painful cash outlay.

8

Second, buy smaller bottles. Most liqueurs can be found in cheaper, half-sized bottles; better yet, many liquor stores sell those tiny, airline-sized 1 1/2 ounce miniatures. You can save an enormous amount of money this way. And avoid an enormous amount of frustration: Why pay $25 for a full liter of Pernod, when the drink you want to make only calls for a scant 1/8 teaspoon of the stuff? Our mini-bottle of Pernod has lasted us for over a year now! This is also the best way to sample a drink you're not sure you'll like; spending a mere couple of dollars on an ingredient you may never use again hurts a lot less, and takes up a lot less space in your bar. Of course, once you discover a drink you'll want to make often, bigger bottles become more economical.

Finally, if you know others who need to expand their hooch horizons, you can divide and conquer: split the cost of a bottle, then split the bottle.

However you swing it, you'll want to economize, because you're about to buy lots of...

RUM

A few tropicals call for gin, brandy, bourbon or okolehao, a Hawaiian spirit distilled from the root of the ti plant. But the vast majority of these drinks are rum-based. And not just rum, but very specific types of rum – often two or more in the same drink, combined to produce a unique, layered, complex flavor that no one rum can approach on its own. Some of these rums are hard to find, but without them you'll never achieve the results you're after.

You'll need two different kinds of JAMAICAN RUM, gold and dark. Gold Jamaican is pale yellow in color and has a subtle, fruity taste. Dark Jamaican is deep brown, with a pungent, full-bodied flavor. Of the many sampled for this book, Lemon Hart was best of show in both categories. It was also the hardest to find. The easiest were Myers's dark and Appleton Special gold. (Appleton also sells a 12-year Special Reserve Jamaican rum that deserves a prominent place on your shelf of "the good stuff.")

DEMERARA RUM is the secret ingredient in most truly memorable tropical drinks, an essential purchase. Made on the island of Guyana, it has a rich, aromatic, smokey flavor. You will need two proofs: normal and 151. Lemon Hart makes the best of both. Fortunately, it's much easier to find than their Jamaican rums; most large liquor stores stock both proofs.

9

By contrast, PUERTO RICAN RUMS seem one-dimensional. But you'll need them to mix with others. Light Puerto Rican is dry and colorless, in more ways than one. Any name brand will do. But for your gold, which is more flavorful than the light, it's worth spending a few extra bucks for Bacardi Reserve or Anejo. (Gold Puerto Rican is actually light brown in color; some distilleries, Bacardi included, label theirs "dark.") Last but not least, always keep some Bacardi 151 handy for your flaming ceremonial offerings.

You can get by quite nicely with just the rums listed above. But when it's time to jog your jaded palate, consider the following:

BARBADOS RUM is gold in color, delicate and refined in taste. Cockspur is good and expensive; Mount Gay is good and cheap.

RHUM BARBANCOURT is an aged Haitian rum with a fine, silky, distinctive flavor. The eight-year-old Five Star mixes best, but the cheaper Three Star will do in a pinch. For big spenders looking for a sipping rum, there's also the Cognac-like, fifteen-year Barbancourt Eight Star.

An important ingredient in Trader Vic's Mai Tai recipe, MARTINIQUE RUM is hard to come by in the U.S., but the best brand – Rhum Saint James – is sporadically available here. It comes in clear and aged amber varieties. If you only want to shell out for one, opt for the amber, although the clear makes for an unusually crisp, drier Mai Tai. Tonier liquor stores and gourmet markets sometimes stock other, more obscure Martinique rums imported from France. Some of these are wonderful, but it's an expensive gamble. Whatever you do, avoid Rhum Negrita, a harsh, candy-like import that gives the entire Caribbean a bad name.

If you can't find any Martinique rum at all, there's still TRADER VIC'S MAI TAI RUM . As of this writing, it's still being bottled by the Trader Vic retailing arm (the newer bottles are labelled "Trader Vic's Caribbean Rum," but it's the same stuff). A blend of Martinique and Jamaican rums, it's an excellent value – cheap and very tasty.

CUBAN RUM is not legally available in the US. But if ever there was a reason to lift the embargo against Castro, this is it: Havana Club, the brand officially exported by the government, is a suberb light rum that puts its Puerto Rican

counterpart to shame. You can buy it in Canada and Mexico; while the Beachbum does not officially condone smuggling, if you should just *happen* to find yourself with a bottle, substitute it for any recipe in this book that calls for light Puerto Rican rum. The difference will have you shouting *"Viva la revolucion"* in no time. And the amber, seven-year-old Havana Club Anejo is so smooth you can drink it straight.

As for other rums you *can* buy here, larger liquor stores now stock a wide variety of imports from Europe, Central and South America, Australia, Bermuda, even the Philippines. There's no compelling reason to buy any of them, with two exceptions:

From England, PUSSER'S NAVY RUM is a hearty blend of six different Caribbean rums. It comes in two strengths; go for the gusto and choose the 95.5 proof Blue Label.

Finally, STROH is an extremely aromatic Austrian rum-based spirit that weighs in at 160 proof. It's used mostly in cooking, but a few drops really wakes up a tired cocktail too. Buy the smallest bottle you can find; a little of this stuff goes a long way.

LIQUEURS

There's no difference between CURACAO and BLUE CURACAO except their color; both are made from dried orange peels, port wine and spices.

Brown and white CREME DE CACAO are also identical, a blend of vanilla and cocoa beans. CREME DE CASSIS is distilled from black currant berries; CREME DE BANANA from bananas and brandy. ("Cremes" are so-called because their high sugar content gives them a cream-like thickness.)

PERNOD is a French, licorice-flavored aperitif that replaced Absinthe when that notorius elixir was banned for turning pre-WWI Paris into a city of literally blind drunks.

BENEDICTINE, also from France, is made by Benedictine monks from a secret formula of herbs and spices they've been distilling since 1510.

COINTREAU and GRAND MARNIER are more delicate, refined liqueurs than TRIPLE SEC, but all three are orange-based.

BARENJAGER is a German honey liqueur; LAIRD'S APPLEJACK, an American apple brandy.

You can pluck all of the above, along with APRICOT BRANDY and PEACH BRANDY, from the shelves of any neighborhood liquor store. But you'll have to cast a wider net for these:

MARASCHINO LIQUEUR is made in the Balkans from marasca cherries and their crushed pits, according to a 400-year-old recipe. Not to be confused with maraschino cocktail cherries.

Likewise, PIMENTO LIQUEUR bears no relation to the pimentos stuffed into olives. Made by Wray & Nephew in Jamaica, this most cordial of cordials has the rich, robust, aromatic flavor of allspice.

ALIZE is the latest in a long line of attempts to market a passion fruit liqueur. In the early '60s, Royal Hawaiian tried to boost sales of their brand by suggesting to housewives that "it also lends itself to fruit compotes or salads." In the '80s, France weighed in with La Grande Passion, but the result tasted like children's cough medicine. Also from France, Alize gets it right this time: It's a light, dry, fragrant blend of cognac and real passion fruit juice.

SYRUPS AND MIXERS

Once upon a time, GRENADINE was a thick, flavorful plasma made from pomegranates. Then Rose's somehow cornered the market with a synthetic sugar water that isn't fit for a hummingbird. Trader Vic's, Fee Brothers, Angostura and Giroux all market far superior grenadines; do everything you can to find them before succumbing to Rose's.

Anyone who has ever tried to dissolve granulated sugar in a drink will praise Pele for SUGAR SYRUP, also known as ROCK CANDY SYRUP or SIMPLE SYRUP. Trader Vic's and Fee Brothers again come to the rescue here. You can also make your own: just boil two pounds of granulated sugar in two cups of water. When the sugar's thoroughly dissolved (after five minutes or so), cool it and bottle it.

FALERNUM is a West Indian sweetener perfumed with exotic spices and fruit extracts. ORGEAT syrup is an almond flavoring made by several companies. As for PASSION FRUIT SYRUP, Trader Vic's is the only brand that actually contains passion fruit. Accept no substitutes!

SWEET & SOUR is basically sugar and lemon juice in a bottle. Buy any brand. But when it comes to COCONUT CREAM, we can only vouch for Lopez.

Pick up a jar of MARASCHINO COCKTAIL CHERRIES. Not just to use the cherries as a garnish, but to use the syrup as a secret drink ingredient – an old tiki bar mixologist's trick.

Another mixologist's secret: HONEY. Heated until clarified, it makes an excellent – and organic – sweetener. In the '30s and '40s, MAPLE SYRUP was a popular drink ingredient. Use only Grade A, 100% Vermont or Canadian maple, *not* adulterated syrups like Log Cabin, Aunt Jemima's or Mrs. Butterworth's.

GINGER BEER is not ginger ale. This bitter soda was a popular mixer in the Victorian-era slings favored by John Bull in far flung outposts of the British Empire. Better grocery stores sell the stuff, but steer clear of the too-strong Jamaican imports and hold out for Cock 'N' Bull brand.

JUICES

Always squeeze your own lime juice. The difference is crucial to the fresh, crisp, "alive" taste you're after. Always squeeze your own lemons too. But concentrated orange and grapefruit juice work just fine, as does canned pineapple juice. As for fruit "nectars," buy Kerns in cans. They make by far the best papaya, peach, mango, and apricot nectars for mixing.

MEASURING

A dash too much of any one ingredient can easily destroy the delicate balance of flavors in a drink, so please measure every ingredient carefully: Don't try to pour 3/4 of an ounce by eye or 1/2 teaspoon by a flip of a wrist. In the words of the Trader himself, "Any guy who goes through a lot of gymnastics behind a bar is just putting on the flash. I've never seen one yet that made good drinks."

13

To simplify the process, here's a conversion chart for the measurements used in this book:

1/4 ounce = 2 teaspoons
1/2 ounce = 1 tablespoon
3/4 ounce = 1/2 jigger, or 1 tablespoon + 2 teaspoons
1 ounce = 2 tablespoons
1 1/2 ounce = 1 jigger
3 ounces = 2 jiggers
8 ounces = 1 cup
32 ounces = 1 quart
25 1/2 ounces = 1 fifth

We've tried to take the guesswork out of measuring by replacing the word "dash" from all recipes, since over the last century bar guides have defined a dash as anything from one drop to a third of an ounce; wherever a dash was called for, we've standardized it to 1/8 teaspoon.

However, we've made an exception for ANGOSTURA BITTERS – the one case where "a flip of the wrist" really *is* the best way to do a dash.

MIXING

Shake too little and you get an unchilled, unblended cocktail. Too much and you get a cold but watery one. Try shaking vigorously for 15 to 20 seconds, or until the outside of your metal shaker frosts. When shaking with ice cubes, use plenty of them. But take care when using crushed ice, which dilutes much faster. A "scoop" should equal one cup of ice, or eight ounces.

SUBSTITUTIONS

They're great if you want to experiment – that's how new drinks are born – but to experience a drink as it was meant to be, stick to what's on the page. If that Suffering Bastard recipe calls for Virgin Islands rum and you put in Old Slatternly, then you've made a different drink. Hasn't the Bastard suffered enough over the years?

HOW TO USE THIS BOOK

On the second-to-last page of this book, our DRINK INDEX breaks down the book's recipes into the following categories: small rum drinks, medium-sized rum drinks, large rum drinks, bourbon drinks, vodka drinks, gin drinks, hot drinks, party punches, and non-alcoholic drinks. Once you've looked up a drink from the index, you'll find a ROW OF SYMBOLS above the recipe that will tell you: 1) how strong the drink is, 2) what kind of vessel to put it in, and 3) whether you'll need a blender or a shaker to make it. For example, the row of symbols

indicates a strong drink served in a skull mug and made with a blender. (If you don't see a blender or shaker icon, just stir vigorously.) Here's a key to all the symbols you'll encounter:

| Light | Medium | Strong | Blender | Shaker |

| Barrel Mug | Champagne Saucer | Cocktail | Coconut Mug | Coffee Mug | Collins | Double Old-Fashioned |

| Easter Island Head Mug | Grapefruit Supreme | Hurricane | Large Snifter | Large Tiki Mug | Medium Snifter | Old-Fashioned |

| Pilsener | Pineapple Shell | Pint | Skull Mug | Small Wine Goblet | Tall Tiki Mug | Tiki Bowl |

ANCIENT MARINER

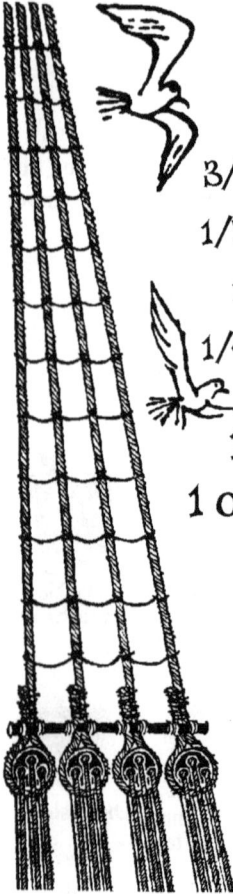

3/4 ounce fresh lime juice
1/2 ounce grapefruit juice
1/2 ounce sugar syrup
1/4 ounce Pimento liqueur

1 ounce Demerara rum
1 ounce dark Jamaican rum

Serve in double old-fashioned glass filled with
crushed ice. Garnish with lime wedge and mint sprig.

Our original creation.

16

ASTRO AKU AKU

1 1/2 ounces fresh lime juice
1 ounce papaya nectar
1/2 ounce apricot nectar
3/4 ounce sugar syrup
1/2 ounce Falernum
Dash Angostura bitters

1 ounce 151 Demerara rum
1 1/2 ounces gold Puerto Rican rum

Blend everything with 1/2 cup crushed ice. Pour into 16 ounce Easter Island mug filled with ice cubes, or large snifter filled with ice cubes.

The height of the Polynesian restaurant craze dovetailed with the advent of the Space Age, and almost every tiki bar named at least one drink in honor of the Final Frontier. The Outrigger served a Flying Saucer, the **Mai Kai** had its Jet Pilot, and even Trader Vic got into the act with his Space Needle. This is our humble addition to the Astro-Aku convergence, based on the Hawaii Kai restaurant's "Sufferin' Bastard." (For an authentic Suffering Bastard, see page 79.)

17

Aurora Bora Borealis

1/2 ounce Lopez coconut cream
1/2 ounce fresh lime juice
1/4 ounce orange juice
Teaspoon orgeat syrup

1 ounce dark Jamaican rum
1 ounce light Puerto Rican rum

Blend with 1/2 cup crushed ice for 15 seconds at low speed. Pour into large cocktail glass.

Our version of the Fern Gully.

18

BEACHCOMBER'S GOLD

1/2 ounce French vermouth
1/2 ounce Italian vermouth
Dash Angostura bitters
1/8 teaspoon Pernod

1 1/2 ounces light Puerto Rican rum

Blend for 5 seconds with 2 ounces crushed ice. Strain into cocktail glass, or into saucer champagne glass with ice shell forming hood over glass:

BEACHCOMBER'S GOLD
ICE SHELL

To prepare mold: Pack finely shaved ice along bottom and sides of glass, forming a hood that projects over glass. Freeze glass overnight. Serve with short straw.

By Don the Beachcomber, whose bartenders spent a lot of their time sculpting ice into fancy forms. It was a big hit with the customers, who delighted in receiving their drinks "sleeping in a cove of ice."

19

BEACHCOMBER'S PUNCH

1/2 ounce fresh lime juice
1/2 ounce grapefruit juice
1/2 ounce apricot brandy
1/2 ounce simple syrup

Dash Angostura bitters
1/8 teaspoon Pernod
1 1/2 ounces Demerara rum

Blend with 6 ounces crushed ice for 5 seconds. Pour into 10 ounce pilsener glass. Add more crushed ice to fill. Garnish with mint sprig.

By Don The Beachcomber, circa 1937. The Angostura/Pernod combination was the Beachcomber's "secret ingredient," used in drinks with dark rum as the base flavor. (Back then Herbsaint was used instead of the similar-tasting Pernod; we've made the substitution because Pernod is far easier to find now.)

BLACKBEARD'S GHOST

1 ounce orange juice
1/2 ounce Falernum
2 ounces sweet & sour
1/2 ounce apricot brandy
2 dashes Angostura bitters
1 1/2 ounces light Puerto Rican rum
1/2 ounce Demerara rum

Mix in cocktail shaker with a glass-full of crushed ice, then pour everything back into glass.

Our version of the Pirate Grog, from Blackbeard's Galley restaurant, Newport Beach, California, circa 1970s, when restaurant critic Paul Wallach called the place "A feisty theme restaurant with decor to match the name."

Blue Hawaii

2 ounces unsweetened
pineapple juice
1 ounce sweet & sour
3/4 ounce Blue Curacao
1/2 teaspoon cream or half & half
1 1/2 ounces vodka

Mix everything in tall glass packed with crushed ice. If you're still feeling blue, try our own creation below:

Blue Reef

1 1/2 ounces
fresh lime juice
1 1/2 ounces Blue Curacao
1/2 ounce Galliano
2 ounces light
Puerto Rican rum

Shake well with ice cubes. Strain into medium snifter filled with crushed ice.

Boo Loo

A few small chunks fresh pineapple
2 1/2 ounces unsweetened pineapple juice
1 1/2 ounces fresh lime juice
1 ounce honey
1 1/2 ounces club soda
1 1/2 ounces Demerara rum
1 1/2 ounces gold Puerto Rican rum
3/4 ounce dark Jamaican rum
3/4 ounce 151 Demerara rum

Heat honey until liquid, then mix with juices and fruit in blender. Stir in rums and soda. Pour into 36 ounce snifter filled with crushed ice, or serve in a hollowed out pineapple:

Boo Loo in a Pineapple

To prepare pineapple shell: Cut off top of pineapple at a slant. Hollow out pineapple center, leaving 1" fruit intact at sides and bottom to hold drink. Fill shell with crushed ice and pour in drink. Replace top of shell and serve with long straw.

Circa 1965.

23

CAPTAIN'S GROG

1/2 ounce fresh lime juice
1/2 ounce grapefruit juice
1/2 ounce maple syrup
1/2 ounce Falernum
1/2 ounce Orange Curacao
1 ounce soda water
3 drops vanilla extract
3 drops almond extract

WELCOME
ABOARD
FINE FOOD
QUALITY SPIRITS

the Captains' Inn
Alamitos Bay
LONG BEACH MARINA

3/4 ounce Myers's rum
1/2 ounce light Puerto Rican rum
1/2 ounce dark Puerto Rican rum

Shake with ice cubes. Strain into double old-fashioned glass filled with crushed ice, or Navy Grog Ice Cone (see page 53 for instructions). Garnish with mint sprig and green cocktail cherry.

From the Captain's Inn, Long Beach, California, circa 1962. We'll never know if the Captain's Inn really was "the Southland's most elegant waterfront restaurant," but it certainly was the largest. The five dining rooms included "exotic dishes from far away places" in the Corinthian Room, entertainment in the Commodore's Lounge, and "quality spirits" upstairs in the Hukilau Polynesian Room.

CASTAWAY

3 ounces unsweetened pineapple juice
3/4 ounce Kahlua
1 1/2 ounces gold Jamaican rum

Shake well with ice cubes. Strain into a 10 ounce Pilsener glass filled with crushed ice. Garnish with maraschino cherry and pineapple wedge stuck on rim of glass.

Based on the Jamaican Dust, from Dorian's Red Hand restaurant, New York City.

CHIEF LAPU LAPU

3 ounces orange juice
3 ounces sweet & sour
1 ounce Trader Vic passion fruit syrup

1 1/2 ounces dark Jamaican rum
1 1/2 ounces light Puerto Rican rum

Shake with ice cubes and pour into large snifter
partly filled with more ice cubes.

Circa 1950s. Who does a guy have to kill to get a drink named after him? In the
case of Chief Lapu Lapu, it was a simple matter of wasting Magellan when the
great Spanish navigator dropped anchor in the Philippines in 1521.

CIRO'S SPECIAL

1 ounce fresh
lime juice
3/4 ounce
creme de cassis
1/4 ounce
Grand Marnier

1 1/2 ounces
dark Jamaican rum

Ciro's

Shake with ice cubes and strain into cocktail glass.

From Ciro's nightclub, Hollywood, California, circa 1940s, when headliners Nat King Cole, Abby Lane and Xavier Cugat made this the Sunset Strip's most glamorous nitery. The building now houses the Comedy Store.

27

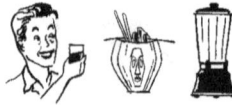

Coconaut

8 ounces Lopez coconut cream
2 ounces fresh lime juice

7 ounces dark Jamaican rum

Put everything into a blender and fill blender to top with ice cubes. Blend until slushy. Pour into ceramic coconut shell mugs. Serves two to four. Ignite drink for a Coconaut Re-entry:

Coconaut Re-Entry

For a flaming Coconaut: Remove pulp from a lime shell, then float shell on surface of drink. Partly fill shell with Bacardi 151 proof rum. Ignite from safe distance with long stem match.

Our original creation.

28

COLONEL BEACH'S PLANTATION PUNCH

1 ounce fresh lime juice

2 ounces unsweetened pineapple juice

1/2 ounce Falernum

2 ounces ginger beer

2 dashes Angostura bitters

1/8 teaspoon Pernod

2 ounces dark Jamaican rum

1 ounce gold Puerto Rican rum

1/2 ounce Barbados rum

Shake with one cup crushed ice. Pour into tall glass with 3 or 4 ice cubes. Garnish with pineapple chunk and sprig of mint.

From Don the Beachcomber's, Honolulu, Hawaii, circa 1950s. When Don divorced his wife Sunny Sund, she got the Hollywood restaurant and he set up shop in Waikiki. In addition to his luau-style Cabaret Restaurant on the beach, he also opened "The Colonel's Plantation Beef Steak And Coffee House" in the International Marketplace. No doubt this drink was invented for the latter.

Coronado Luau Special

4 ounces orange juice
4 ounces sweet & sour
1/4 ounce orgeat syrup

1 ounce dark Jamaican rum
1 ounce light Puerto Rican rum
1/2 ounce Grand Marnier
1/2 ounce brandy

Blend with 1 cup crushed ice for several seconds.
Pour into large tiki mug or tall glass.

By Bert Chan of the Luau Room, Hotel Del Coronado, San Diego, California, circa 1962. Host to Teddy Roosevelt and location of the film *Some Like It Hot*, the Del Coronado was built in 1888. It's still there, but the Luau Room is now a sports bar.

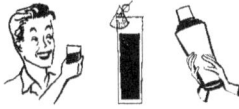

CRUZANA

2 ounces grapefruit juice
3/4 ounce syrup from maraschino
cocktail cherry jar

2 ounces Cruzan Gold rum
or Barbados rum

Shake with ice cubes and pour into Collins glass.

By the Cruzan Rum company, circa 1960s.

DERBY DAIQUIRI

1 ounce orange juice
1/2 ounce fresh lime juice
1/2 ounce sugar syrup

1 1/2 ounces
light Puerto Rican rum

MAI-KAI

Blend with a handful of crushed ice for 15 seconds.
Serve in small wine goblet.

From the Mai Kai restaurant, Fort Lauderdale, Florida, circa 1966. Still going strong, the Mai Kai is the most perfectly preserved and beautifully appointed Polynesian palace left in America. A must if you're anywhere in the Southeastern seaboard.

Don's Own Planter's

1 ounce fresh lemon juice
1 ounce soda water
2 dashes Angostura bitters
1 ounce honey mix
(1 part honey and 1 part water)*

1 1/2 ounces dark Jamaican rum
1 ounce light Puerto Rican rum

Shake with ice cubes and pour everything into Pilsener glass.
Garnish with mint, cherry, and pineapple finger.
* To prepare honey mix, heat 1/2 cup honey until liquid, then
add 1/2 cup water. You can store the leftover mix in the
fridge -- it stays liquid! Or you can use it in one of these:

Don's Daiquiri

3/4 ounce fresh lime juice
3/4 ounce honey mix
2 ounces light Puerto Rican rum

"Shake like hell" with ice cubes and strain into saucer
champagne glass.

Both by Don The Beachcomber, Honolulu, Hawaii, circa 1950.

33

EASTERN SOUR

Juice of 1/2 orange
Juice of 1/2 lemon
1/4 ounce orgeat syrup
1/4 ounce rock candy syrup

2 ounces rye or Bourbon

Serve in double old-fashioned glass filled with crushed ice and one segment each spent orange and lemon shells.

By Trader Vic.

34

FLAMING COFFEE GROG

3 teaspoons Lopez coconut cream
1/4 ounce Grand Marnier
Hot black coffee
Twist of orange peel
Twist of lemon peel
2 whole cloves
Eight-inch cinnamon stick
3/4 ounce 151 Demerara rum

Heat and then ignite cloves, peels, Grand Marnier and rum in Pyrex saucepan or blazer pan of chafing dish. Fill mug 3/4 full of hot coffee, then stir in coconut cream. Spoon flaming mixture on top. Use cinnamon stick as stirrer.

Circa 1950s.

FOG CUTTER

2 ounces fresh lemon juice
1 ounce orange juice
1/2 ounce orgeat syrup
2 ounces light Puerto Rican rum
1 ounce brandy
1/2 ounce gin
1/2 ounce sweet sherry

Shake everything – *except* sherry – with ice cubes.
Pour into tall tiki mug. Add more ice cubes to fill.
Float sherry on top of drink. Serve with straws and
swizzle stick.

Trader Vic on his creation: "Fog Cutter, hell. After two of these, you won't even
see the stuff."

GOLD CUP

3/4 ounce fresh lime juice
3/4 ounce sugar syrup
1/2 ounce
Maraschino liqueur
Teaspoon Pernod
3 drops
almond extract

1 ounce gold
Jamaican rum

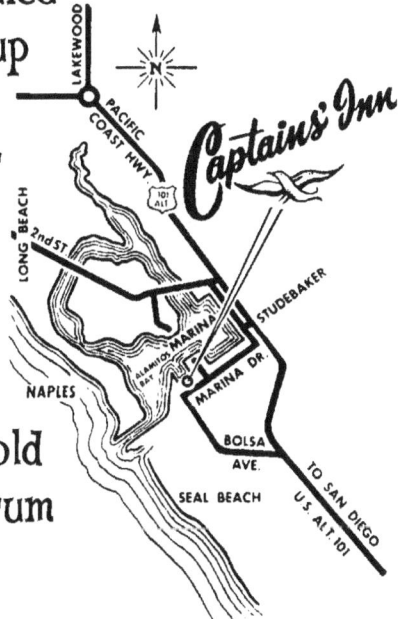

Shake well with ice cubes and strain into saucer champagne glass. This was originally served with an ice shell forming a hood over the glass (see page 19 for instructions).

From the Captain's Inn, Long Beach, California, circa 1962 (see page 24).

Gone The Beachcomber

1 ounce fresh lime juice
1/4 ounce fresh lemon juice
1/2 ounce Trader Vic
passion fruit syrup

1/4 ounce Maraschino liqueur
1/4 ounce sugar syrup

1 ounce
Demerara rum

1/4 ounce
151 Demerara rum

Shake everything – *except* 151 rum – with ice and
strain into 4 ounce cocktail glass. Then float 151.

Our version of the Demerara Dry Float.

38

HAWAII KAI TREASURE

2 ounces fresh lime juice
1 ounce grapefruit juice
1/2 ounce light cream
or half & half
1/2 ounce curacao
1/2 ounce orgeat syrup
1/2 ounce honey
1 1/2 ounces light
Puerto Rican rum

Heat honey until liquid, then whip with all other ingredients and 1 cup crushed ice in blender. Pour over ice cubes in grapefruit supreme glass or tiki bowl. Garnish with gardenia. (The "Treasure" was an 8-mm. pearl hidden among the gardenia petals.)

By Manny "Blackie" Andal of the Hawaii Kai restaurant, New York City, circa 1960s. Located "In the Heart of the Theatrical World" at Broadway and 50th, the now defunct Hawaii Kai beckoned foot traffic with an outdoor waterfall just off the sidewalk. Inside, The Lounge Of The Seven Pleasures offered "Authentic Native Entertainment," while the Okole Maluna Bar featured a Diamond Head diorama with dawn-to-dusk lighting changes.

39

Hawaiian Room

1/2 ounce fresh lemon juice
1/2 ounce pineapple juice
1/2 ounce Applejack
1/2 ounce triple sec

1 ounce light Puerto Rican rum

Shake with plenty of ice cubes until very cold. Strain into cocktail glass.

From the Hawaiian Room of the Hotel Lexington, New York City, New York, circa 1940s. At the time, **Managing Director Charles E. Rochester** lured the smart set to "the famous Hawaiian Room" with "an authentic setting complete even to a tropical rainstorm." There was also a dance floor, live Hawaiian music, and "the famed Lexington cuisine."

40

HEADHUNTER

1 1/4 ounces fresh lime juice
1 1/4 ounces papaya nectar
1/2 ounce peach nectar
3/4 ounce honey
Dash Angostura bitters

1 1/2 ounces Demerara rum
1 ounce 151 Demerara rum
3/4 ounce gold Puerto Rican rum

Heat honey until liquid, then mix with juices and 1/2 cup crushed ice in blender. Stir in rums and bitters. Pour into glass full of ice cubes.

By Manny "Blackie" Andal of the Hawaii Kai restaurant, New York City, circa 1960s. Broadway columnist Earl Wilson was a big fan of the Hawaii Kai, of which he wrote: "The bare-legged, shapely waitresses and rum drinks in intimate Polynesian atmosphere would enable one to celebrate even a headache. Ask for the sentimental proprietor, 'Cryin' Joe' Kipness, who weeps at stripteasers, and he may give you the place."

Hell in The Pacific

3/4 ounce fresh lime juice
1/2 ounce Maraschino liqueur
1/4 ounce grenadine

1 1/2 ounces 151 Demerara rum

Shake well with one scoop crushed ice. Pour
everything into 10 ounce Pilsener glass. Decorate
with American and Japanese flags stuck into lime
wedge on rim of glass.

Our version of the Myrtle Bank Punch, a popular drink in the 1930s.

HURRICANE

2 ounces fresh lemon juice
2 ounces passion fruit syrup

4 ounces dark Jamaican rum

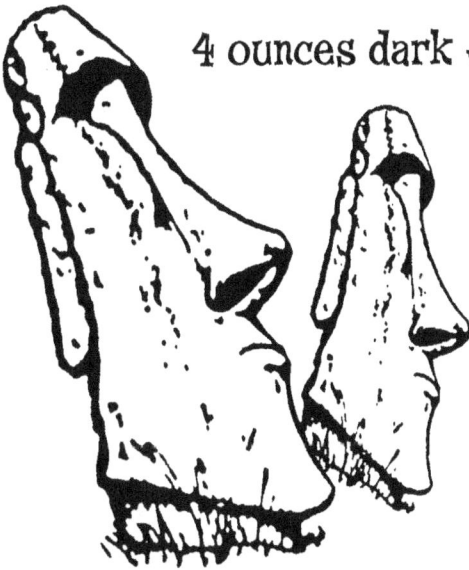

Pour into 20 ounce Hurricane glass or large tiki mug
filled with crushed ice.

From Pat O'Brien's restaurant, New Orleans, Louisiana, circa 1960s. Although
Pat O'Brien's is not a Polynesian restaurant, its Hurricane was widely copied by
tiki bars from coast to coast. Pat had the last laugh, because *his* place is still
here today.

JASPER'S JAMAICAN

1/2 ounce fresh lime juice
1/2 ounce Pimento liqueur
1/4 teaspoon sugar

1 1/4 ounces gold Jamaican rum

Dissolve sugar in lime juice, then shake everything well with ice cubes. Strain into cocktail glass.

By Jasper LeFranc of the Bay Roc Hotel, Montego Bay, Jamaica, circa 1970s.

KAPU-KAI

1/2 ounce fresh lime juice
1/2 ounce sugar syrup
1 ounce 151 Demerara rum

Shake with ice cubes and strain into cocktail glass. If you've still got your sea legs after this one, try Don The Beachcomber's similar but even stronger 1940s-era concoction:

151 SWIZZLE

1/2 ounce fresh lime juice
1/2 ounce sugar syrup
1/8 teaspoon Pernod
Dash Angostura bitters
Ground nutmeg
1 1/2 ounces 151 Demerara rum

Blend with one cup crushed ice for 5 seconds. Pour into Pilsener glass (this was originally served in a 10 ounce metal cup with a flared top, but good luck finding one). Add more crushed ice to fill, top with a shake of ground nutmeg, and garnish with a cinnamon stick.

KRAKATOA

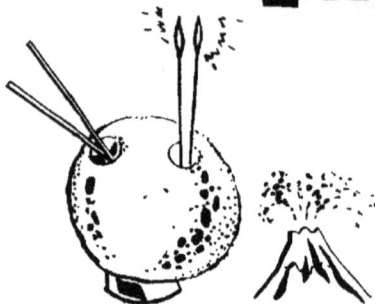

1 1/2 ounces fresh lime juice
1 ounce orange juice
1 ounce grapefruit juice
1 ounce apricot nectar
1/2 ounce Falernum
Teaspoon coffee liqueur
Dash Angostura bitters
1 1/2 ounces gold Puerto Rican rum
1 1/2 ounces Demerara rum
2 ounces chilled Kona coffee

Mix all ingredients – *except* Kona coffee – with 1 cup crushed ice in blender. Pour into 36 ounce snifter filled with ice cubes. Float coffee.

A Hawaii Kai Swizzle with a coffee infusion.

46

LA FLORIDA

1 ounce fresh lime juice
1/2 ounce Italian vermouth
1/4 ounce white creme de cacao
Teaspoon Curacao
Teaspoon grenadine

1 ounce light Puerto Rican rum

Shake with ice cubes and strain into saucer champagne glass. Garnish with twist of orange peel.

By Constantine Ribailagua of the La Florida bar, Havana, Cuba, circa 1930s. Constantine was also renowned for his *Papa Dobles* Daiquiris, named after "Papa" Ernest Hemingway, who consumed them in prodigious numbers during his years in Cuba. (To make one, frappe 4 ounces light rum, 1/4 ounce maraschino liqueur, and the juice of 2 limes and 1/2 grapefruit in a blender full of crushed ice.)

LANI-HONI

1 1/2 ounces Benedictine
1/2 ounce fresh lemon juice

1 ounce light Puerto Rican rum

Matson Lines®

Gently stir with ice cubes in mixing glass, then strain
into a small wine goblet filled with crushed ice.

As served aboard the Matson Line's SS Mariposa on its 42-day South Seas
cruise, circa 1962. Four Matson Liners once "plied the blue Pacific" in "yacht-
like voyages to ports of paradise," sailing from San Francisco to Bora Bora,
Tahiti, Rarotonga, Fiji, Pago Pago, New Caledonia and New Zealand.

48

LYCHEE NUT DAIQUIRI

3 whole canned lychee nuts
1 ounce fresh lime juice
1/4 ounce Maraschino liqueur
1/4 ounce rock candy syrup

1 1/2 ounces light
Puerto Rican rum

Blend with 12 ounces crushed ice until frapped, then pour into large cocktail glasses. Serves two.

By Trader Vic.

49

MAI TAI

1 1/2 ounces fresh lime juice
1/2 ounce Curacao
1/4 ounce orgeat syrup
1/4 ounce rock candy syrup

1 ounce
aged Jamaican rum
1 ounce Martinique rum

Trader Vic

Serve in double old-fashioned glass filled with
crushed ice and spent lime shell.
Garnish with mint sprig.

**Trader Vic on the Mai Tai: "Anyone who says I didn't create this drink
is a dirty stinker."**

MANGO COOLER

3 ounces mango nectar
1 1/2 ounces orange juice
1/2 ounce fresh lemon juice
1/2 ounce Cointreau
1 1/2 ounces vodka

Shake with ice cubes and pour into tall glass. Garnish
with orange slice.

By Thomas Mario, food and drink editor of *Playboy* magazine, circa 1966.

MISSIONARY'S DOWNFALL

4 whole fresh
sprigs of mint
1/2 slice
fresh pineapple
1 1/2 ounces fresh
lime juice
1/2 ounce peach brandy
1/4 ounce sugar syrup
1 ounce light
Puerto Rican rum

THE ORIGINAL
DON THE
BEACHCOMBER

Strip mint leaves from sprigs. Discard stems. Place leaves in blender with all other ingredients and 14 ounces crushed ice. Blend until smooth. Pour into hurricane glass or tall tiki mug.

By Don the Beachcomber, circa 1948, when one of these cost the princely sum of 85 cents.

52

NAVY GROG

3/4 ounce lime juice
3/4 ounce grapefruit juice
3/4 ounce honey

1 ounce light Puerto Rican rum
1 ounce dark Jamaican rum
1 ounce Demerara rum
1 ounce chilled club soda

Heat honey until liquid, then mix with juices in blender. Stir in rums and soda. Pour into double old-fashioned glass filled with crushed ice, or sip drink through ice cone:

NAVY GROG ICE CONE

To prepare cone: pack ten ounce Pilsener glass with finely shaved ice. Run a hole through center with a chopstick to make a passage for straw. Gently remove cone from glass and freeze overnight.

By Don the Beachcomber.

NEVER SAY DIE

1/2 ounce fresh lime juice
1/2 ounce orange juice
1/2 ounce grapefruit juice
1/4 ounce unsweetened
pineapple juice
1/2 ounce honey
Dash Angostura bitters

1 ounce Barbados rum
1/2 ounce light Puerto Rican rum
1/2 ounce dark Jamaican rum

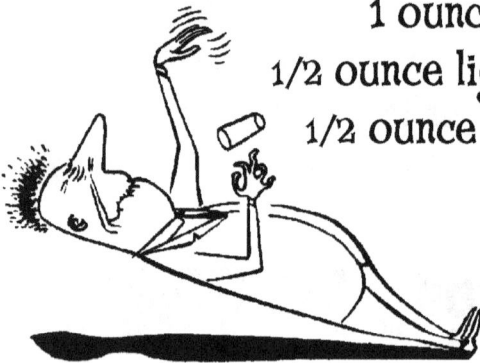

Heat honey until liquid, then blend with all other
ingredients with 4 ounces crushed ice for 5 seconds.
Pour into small wine goblet.

By Don the Beachcomber.

Noa Noa

1 ounce fresh lime juice
Tablespoon brown sugar
Dash angostura bitters
4 to 6 mint leaves

3 ounces Demerara rum

Dissolve sugar in lime juice, then swizzle everything in double old-fashioned glass partially filled with crushed ice. Add more crushed ice to fill. Swizzle again until glass frosts. Garnish with mint sprig and lime shell.

We based this on the Queen's Park Swizzle, from the Queen's Park Hotel, Trinidad, circa 1940s.

OCEANIC PUNCH

3/4 ounce fresh lime juice
3/4 ounce orange juice
3/4 ounce grapefruit juice
3/4 ounce sweet & sour
1/2 ounce sugar syrup

1 1/2 ounces light Puerto Rican rum

Shake well with ice cubes, then pour everything into tall glass. Garnish with Maraschino cherry.

By Dean Short of the Ports O' Call restaurant, Tuscon, Arizona, circa 1960s.

OUTRIGGER

3/4 ounce fresh lemon juice
3/4 ounce triple sec
sugar

1 1/2 ounces Barbados rum

Rub rim of cocktail glass with spent lemon shell, then
coat moistened rim with sugar. Shake juice, triple sec
and rum with ice cubes, then strain into
sugar-frosted glass.

A rum Sidecar.

PAGO PAGO

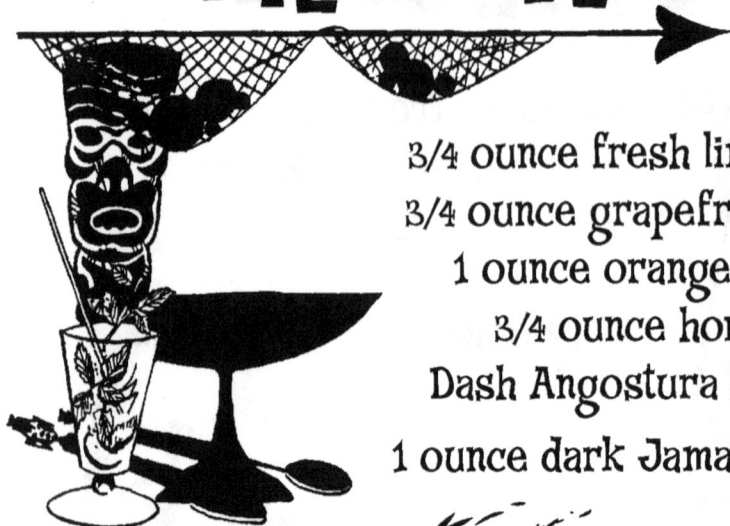

3/4 ounce fresh lime juice
3/4 ounce grapefruit juice
1 ounce orange juice
3/4 ounce honey
Dash Angostura bitters
1 ounce dark Jamaican rum

Blend without ice and pour into Pilsener glass filled with crushed ice.

From the Pago Pago restaurant, Tuscon, Arizona, circa 1963.

PAINKILLER

4 ounces unsweetened
pineapple juice
1 ounce
orange juice
1 ounce Lopez
coconut cream

2 ounces 95 proof
Pusser's rum

Powdered cinnamon
Ground nutmeg

Blend without ice and pour into tall glass or tiki mug
filled with crushed ice. Top with a shake of nutmeg
and a pinch of cinnamon. Garnish with pineapple stick,
orange wheel, and cinnamon stick.

By the Pusser's rum company. "Pusser" is 18th century British Naval slang for
"Purser," the ship's officer responsible for doling out the crew's daily rum ration.

PALACE COURT

3/4 ounce fresh lime juice
1/4 ounce sugar syrup

1 ounce Five-star Rhum Barbancourt

Shake with ice cubes and strain into cocktail glass.

Our original creation.

PIECES OF EIGHT

1 1/2 ounces fresh lemon juice

1/2 ounce fresh lime juice

1 1/2 ounces Trader Vic
passion fruit syrup

1 1/2 ounces light
Puerto Rican rum

Blend with 1/2 cup crushed ice for several seconds
and pour into tall glass. Add more crushed ice to fill.

From the Pieces Of Eight restaurant, Marina Del Rey, California, circa 1962.
Back then the house band was Paul Page and The Island-Aires, whose numbers
included: "When Sam Goes Back To Samoa," "Chicken Kona Kai," and "Big Luau
In The Sky," which is where the Pieces Of Eight went by the '70s.

61

PLANET OF THE APES

3/4 ounce
Creme de Banana
1 ounce unsweetened
pineapple juice
1 ounce orange juice
1/2 ounce fresh lime juice

2 ounces dark Jamaican rum

Shake with 1 cup crushed ice. Pour everything into 10 ounce Pilsener glass. Garnish with fresh banana slice speared to Maraschino cherry.

From a West Indian punch recipe.

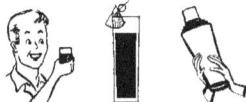

PLANTER'S PUNCH

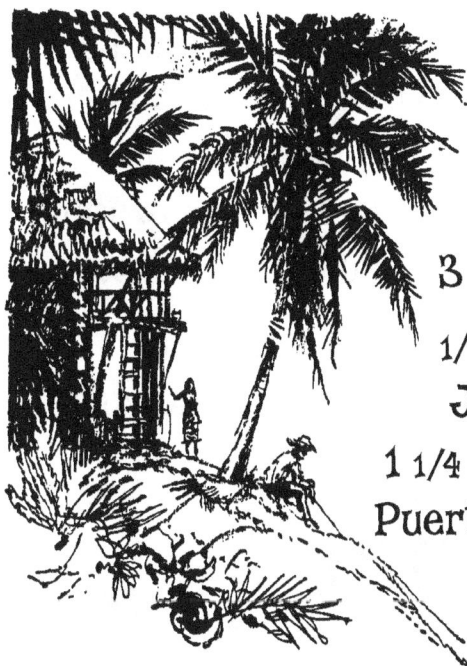

1 1/4 ounces
orange juice
1 1/4 ounces fresh
lemon juice
3 teaspoons grenadine
1/2 ounce dark
Jamaican rum
1 1/4 ounces light
Puerto Rican rum

Shake everything – *except* dark Jamaican rum – with scoop of crushed ice and pour into tall glass. Then float dark Jamaican on top of drink. Garnish with orange slice and Maraschino cherry speared to pineapple chunk.

From the Polo Lounge of the Beverly Hills hotel, Beverly Hills, California, circa 1960s.

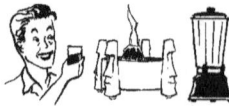

POLYNESIAN PARALYSIS

3 ounces orange juice
3 ounces unsweetened
pineapple juice
1 ounce sweet & sour
1/2 ounce orgeat syrup

3 ounces Okolehao
or Martinique rum

Blend with 12 ounces crushed ice for 5 seconds. Pour into tiki bowl and garnish with an orchid. Serve with long straw.

In his 1960 book *Waikiki Beachnik*, H. Allen Smith diagnosed the symptoms of Polynesian Paralysis as "a screaming desire not to work, not to do anything that requires any substantial effort either physical or mental." The most extreme case might well be that of the Duke of Windsor, who caught the disease, then known as "Waikiki Pip," in 1920 ... and went on to renounce the throne of England.

POLYNESIAN SPELL

1 ounce grape juice
Juice of 1/2 lemon
1/4 ounce triple sec
1/4 ounce peach brandy
1/2 teaspoon sugar

1 1/2 ounces dry gin

Dissolve sugar in lemon juice, then shake all ingredients with ice cubes and strain into champagne glass.

By Sandro Conti of the Kahiki restaurant, Columbus, Ohio, circa 1961. His advice back then: "If it still doesn't taste like the Kahiki's, add a pinch of romance." Although this drink hasn't been on the menu for decades, the Kahiki is still open; its three-stories-tall Easter Island head fireplace must be seen to be believed. Apparently the Federal Government agrees, because the Kahiki was recently listed on the National Register of Historic Places.

PORT LIGHT

1 ounce fresh lemon juice
1/2 ounce passion fruit syrup
3 teaspoons grenadine

1 ounce Bourbon

Blend with 1 cup crushed ice for 5 seconds and pour into collins glass or nautical tumbler. Add more crushed ice to fill.

To make a Starboard Light, substitute Scotch for Bourbon.

Q.B. COOLER

1/2 ounce fresh lime juice
1/2 ounce orange juice
1/4 ounce passion fruit syrup
1/4 ounce sugar syrup
2 ounces dark Jamaican rum
1 ounce light Puerto Rican rum
Dash Angostura bitters
1/8 teaspoon Pernod

Blend with 12 ounces crushed ice for 5 seconds and pour into double old-fashioned glass. Add more crushed ice to fill. Garnish with mint sprigs.

By Don the Beachcomber, circa 1941, when the house rule was "a limit of two to a customer."

RED TIDE

3/4 ounce fresh
lime juice
1/2 ounce grenadine

1 ounce gold
Jamaican rum

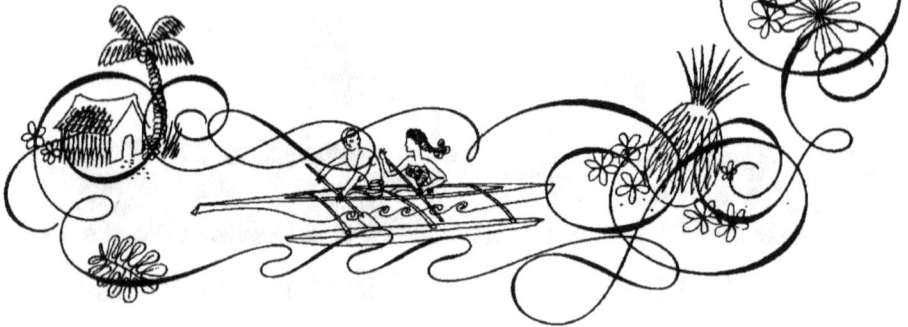

Shake with ice cubes and strain into cocktail glass.

Our orginal creation.

THE REEF

1/2 ounce fresh lime juice
1/2 ounce triple sec
1/2 ounce
passion fruit liqueur (Alize)

1 ounce light Puerto Rican rum

Shake with ice. Strain into saucer champagne glass
containing one ice cube.

From the Reef restaurant, Long Beach, California, circa 1962. Quoth the
management: "Like a reef, there is a dangerous element lying under the cooling
surface of this one."

ROYAL HAWAIIAN

1 1/2 ounces pineapple juice
1/2 ounce fresh lemon juice
Teaspoon orgeat syrup

1 1/2 ounces gin

Shake with ice cubes and strain into chilled
cocktail glass.

From the Moana Hotel, Honolulu, Hawaii, circa 1948. Webley Edwards' then-famous radio program *Hawaii Calls*, featuring the Singing Surfriders and the Waikiki Maidens, was often broadcast live from the Banyan Court of the Moana; up to 3,000 middle-aged tourists at a time would pack the courtyard to hear Edwards open the show with his trademark "Aloha," to which the crowd would always respond, "a-LO-ha!" Of all the primitive tribal rituals of Polynesia, this may well have been the strangest.

RUM BARREL

3/4 ounce fresh lime juice
3/4 ounce orange juice
3/4 ounce unsweetened
pineapple juice
3/4 ounce Alize
passion fruit liqueur
3/4 ounce sugar syrup

3/4 ounce dark
Jamaican rum
3/4 ounce
Bacardi 151 rum

Shake with ice cubes and pour into
ceramic barrel mug.

Adapted from a recipe by Dean Short of the Ports O' Call restaurant,
Tuscon, Arizona, circa 1960s.

71

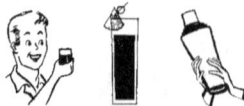

RUM LIFT

2 ounces orange juice
1/2 ounce unsweetened pineapple juice
1/4 ounce fresh lime juice
Dash Angostura bitters

1 1/2 ounces dark Jamaican rum

Shake with 1 cup crushed ice, pour into tall glass.
Garnish with Maraschino cherry and pineapple spear.

By Ray Fine of Don The Beachcomber's, Hollywood, California, circa 1968,
when this was served as a hangover cure.

72

RUM RUNNER

1 1/2 ounces fresh lime juice
7/8 ounce blackberry brandy
7/8 ounce creme de banana
5/8 ounce grenadine

3/4 ounce Bacardi 151 rum

Pour everything into blender and fill blender 1/2 full
with ice cubes. Blend until smooth. Pour into pint
glass or large tiki mug.

By "Tiki John" Ebert of the Holiday Isle Resort, Islamorada, Florida Keys,
1972. At that time customers would mix their own drinks from bottles left out
on the bar; Ebert cobbled together the Rum Runner from leftover ingredients –
and created a drink so popular it now has its own T-shirt at the
Holiday Isle gift shop.

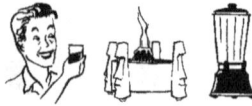

SCORPION BOWL

6 ounces orange juice
4 ounces fresh lemon juice
1 1/2 ounces orgeat syrup

6 ounces light Puerto Rican rum
1 ounce brandy

Blend with 2 cups crushed ice and pour into tiki bowl.
Add ice cubes to fill. Garnish with a gardenia.
Serves 2 to 4.

Over the years Trader Vic modified his Scorpion several times, but this '60s-era
version became the standard. For the record, here is his original 1940s recipe:
1 ounce Peruvian Pisco brandy, 10 ounces light rum, 4 ounces lemon juice, 2
ounces orange juice, 2 ounces orgeat, shake with cracked ice and serve as above.

SHARK'S TOOTH

1/2 ounce fresh lime juice
1/2 ounce unsweetened pineapple juice
1/2 ounce sugar syrup
Teaspoon syrup from
maraschino cherry jar
1 ounce Barbados rum
1 ounce 12-year Appleton Special Reserve rum

Blend everything -- *except* 12-year Appleton -- with 3 ounces crushed ice. Pour into 6 ounce old fashioned glass. Stir in Appleton. Sip without straw.

SHRUNKEN SKULL

1 ounce fresh lime juice
1 ounce grenadine
1 ounce gold Puerto Rican rum
1 ounce Demerara rum

Shake vigorously with ice cubes, then pour everything into skull mug.

Mid-century exotica didn't just cater to suburban fantasies of work-free islands and guilt-free sex. There was also the call of adventure, epitomized by these two classic "dangerous" drinks: If the sharks didn't eat you, the cannibals would!

SIDEWINDER'S FANG

1 1/2 ounces fresh lime juice
1 1/2 ounces orange juice
1 1/2 ounces passion fruit syrup
3 ounces club soda
1 ounce dark Jamaican rum
1 ounce Demerara rum

THE LANAI

Blend with 1/2 cup crushed ice for 10 seconds. Pour into large snifter filled with ice cubes. Garnish with length of spiral-cut orange peel.

From the Lanai restaurant, San Mateo, California, circa 1960s. There may have been more elaborate Polynesian palaces, but only the Lanai held the distinction of operating its own tiki-themed liquor store down the street.

SINGAPORE SLING

1 ounce fresh lime juice
1 ounce cherry brandy
1/2 ounce Benedictine
1/2 ounce brandy
2 ounces gin
1 1/2 ounces club soda

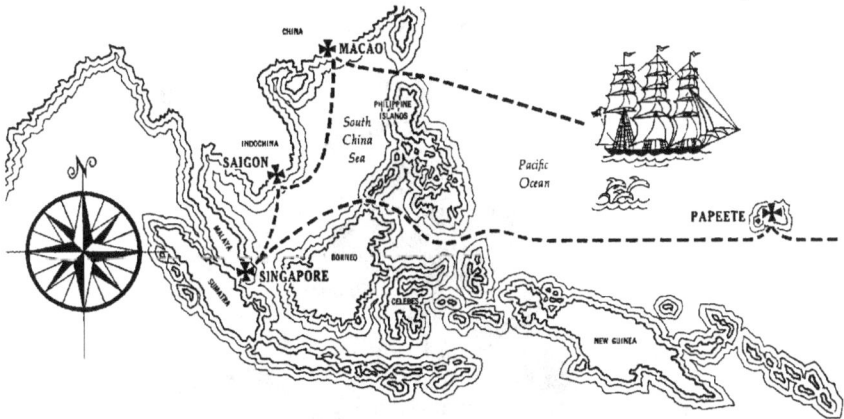

Shake everything – *except* soda – with ice cubes and strain into Collins glass. Top with soda. Add ice cubes to fill. Stir. Garnish with orange wheel and mint sprig.

From the **Raffles Hotel**, Singapore, circa early 1900s. The word sling may have originated from the German "schlingen," which means "to swallow."

77

SPINDRIFT

3 ounces orange juice
2 ounces fresh lemon juice
1 ounce passion fruit syrup
3/4 ounce sugar syrup
1/2 teaspoon vanilla extract
2 ounces dark Jamaican rum
1 1/2 ounces Demerara rum
1 ounce light Puerto Rican rum

Blend with 2 1/2 cups crushed ice and pour into large snifter.

Based on the **Rum Pot**, by Trader Vic.

SUFFERING BASTARD

1 ounce fresh
lime juice
4 ounces chilled
ginger ale

Dash Angostura bitters

1 ounce Bourbon
1 ounce gin

Pour everything into double old-fashioned glass and fill glass with ice cubes. Stir well. Garnish with mint sprig and orange wheel speared with maraschino cherry.

From Shepheard's Hotel, Cairo, Egypt, circa 1950. Legend has it that at the turn of the century, on a sweltering rush hour at Shepheard's bar, some British officers misheard the bartender's comment about his "poor, suffering bar steward" – and christened this drink (made back then with brandy and ginger beer in place of Bourbon and ginger ale) the "Suffering Bastard."

TAHITIAN

1 1/2 ounces unsweetened
pineapple juice
1 ounce fresh lime juice
1/2 ounce white creme de cacao
1/2 teaspoon sugar syrup
Dash Angostura bitters
2 ounces Rhum Barbancourt
1 1/2 ounces gold Jamaican rum
1/2 ounce gold Puerto Rican rum

Shake with ice cubes, then pour everything into a
collins glass. Garnish with pineapple wedge stuck to
rim of glass. Stick paper parasol into
pineapple wedge.

Our original creation.

TASMAN SEA

1 ounce fresh lime juice
3/4 ounce fresh lemon juice
1/4 ounce orange curacao
2 tablespoons brown sugar

1 ounce 151 Puerto Rican rum
1/2 ounce 151 Demerara rum

Dissolve sugar in lime juice. Blend everything –
except Demerara – with 10 ounces crushed ice for 10
seconds. Pour into large snifter. Stir in Demerara.

Our version of the Lady Love.

TEST PILOT

1/2 ounce fresh lime juice
1/2 ounce Falernum
3 teaspoons Cointreau

Dash Angostura bitters
1/8 teaspoon Pernod

3/4 ounce light Puerto Rican rum
1 1/2 ounces dark Jamaican rum

Blend with 1 cup crushed ice for 5 seconds, then pour into double old-fashioned glass. Add more crushed ice to fill. Garnish with a wooden oyster fork with maraschino cherry skewered on prongs.

By Don the Beachcomber, circa 1941.

82

TORTUGA

1/2 ounce orange juice
1/2 ounce fresh lemon juice
1/2 ounce fresh lime juice
1 ounce Italian vermouth
1/2 ounce Curacao
1/2 ounce creme de cacao
1/4 ounce grenadine
1 ounce 151 Demerara rum
3/4 ounce 151 Bacardi rum

Shake with ice cubes. Strain into Pilsener glass filled
with crushed ice. Drop in lime wedge to garnish.

By Trader Vic, circa 1948. We've substituted Bacardi for the ounce of 123
proof Cuban rum called for in the original.

TRADE WIND COCKTAIL

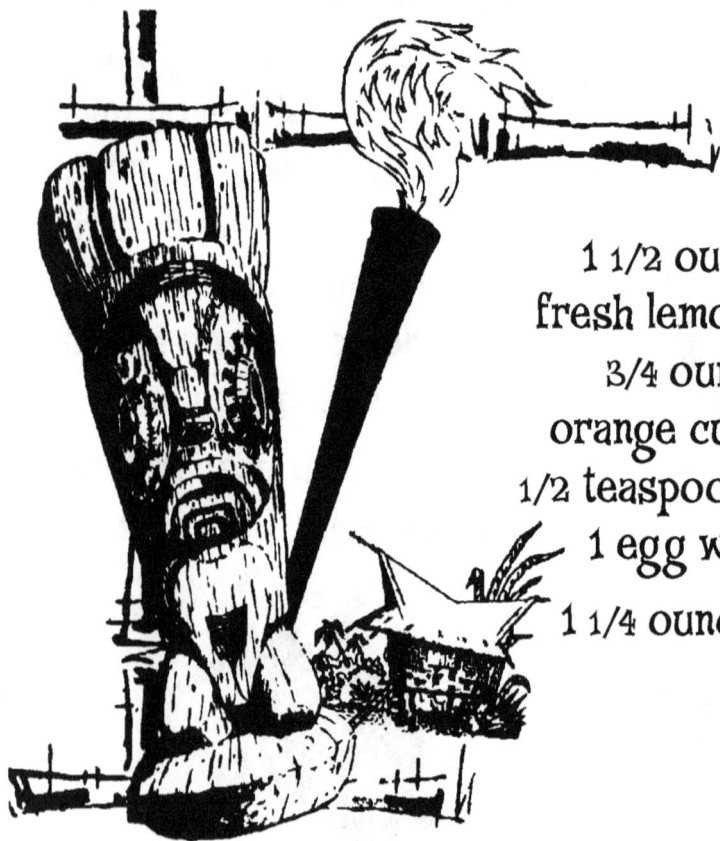

1 1/2 ounces
fresh lemon juice
3/4 ounce
orange curacao
1/2 teaspoon sugar
1 egg white
1 1/4 ounce gin

Dissolve sugar in lemon juice, then shake everything with plenty of ice cubes. Strain into chilled cocktail glass.

From the Trade Winds restaurant, Watermill, Long Island, circa 1959.

TRADER VIC GROG

1 ounce unsweetened
pineapple juice
1 ounce lemon juice
1 ounce Trader Vic
passion fruit syrup
Dash Angostura bitters

2 ounces dark Jamaican rum

Serve in tiki mug filled with crushed ice.
Garnish with mint sprig.

By Trader Vic.

Volcano House
Hot Buttered Rum

3/4 ounce fresh
lemon juice
1/4 ounce
Maraschino liqueur
3/4 ounce
sugar
Hot tea
Butter
Cloves
1 1/2 ounces Myers's rum

Pour juice, Maraschino, sugar and rum into mug. Fill rest of mug with very hot tea. Stir well, then float small piece of butter. Add twist of lemon peel and 3 or 4 cloves.

By Bob Ida, Head Bartender, Volcano House Hotel, Hawaii National Park, circa 1950. Perched on the rim of the Kilauea Crater, the Volcano House still offers great views of the Big Island's active volcano, but it no longer offers this drink.

VON TIKI

1 ounce Barenjager
1/2 teaspoon Stroh
3/4 ounce fresh
lime juice

1 ounce
Barbados rum

Shake with ice cubes and strain into cocktail glass.

Our orginal creation.

WAIKIKIAN

1 1/2 ounces fresh lemon juice
1 ounce Curacao
3/4 ounce orgeat syrup

1 1/2 ounces light
Puerto Rican rum

1 1/2 ounces
dark Jamaican rum

Blend everything – *except* dark Jamaican rum – with 3 ounces crushed ice. Pour into double old-fashioned glass 2/3 filled with crushed ice. Float dark Jamaican on top of drink. Garnish with orchid and lime wheel.

Based on the Island Hopper, circa 1960.

88

ZOMBIE

1 ounce fresh lime juice
3/4 ounce unsweetened
pineapple juice
3/4 ounce papaya nectar
1/2 ounce Applejack
Tablespoon powdered sugar

GREETINGS:
FROM DON THE BEACHCOMBER'S
WHERE GOOD RUM IS
IMMORTALIZED AND DRINKING
IS AN ART

1 ounce dark Jamaican rum
2 ounces Barbados rum
1 ounce light Puerto Rican rum
1/2 ounce 151 Demerara rum

Shake everything – *except* Demerara – with ice cubes. Pour into tall glass. Float Demerara on top of drink. Garnish with mint sprig, pineapple cube skewered between red and green cocktail cherries, and a pinch more powdered sugar sprinkled over all.

An anonymous 1934 attempt to reproduce Don The Beachcomber's "often imitated, never duplicated" recipe. The story goes that Don whipped this up on the spot to revive a hung-over businessman (see page 5). But the copy from a 1941 Beachcomber menu offers a different origin myth: "The Zombie didn't just happen. It is the result of a long and expensive process of evolution ... In the experiments leading up to the Zombie, three and a half cases of assorted rums were used and found their way down the drain so that you may now enjoy this potent 'mender of broken dreams'."

Party Punches
&
Non-Alcoholic
Drinks

BARBANCOURT RUM CUP

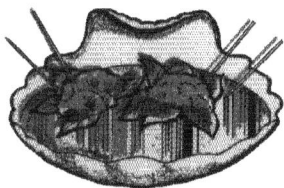

2/3 cup fresh lime juice
2/3 cup orgeat syrup
2 dashes Angostura bitters

1 fifth Barbancourt 3-Star or 5-Star rum

Combine in pitcher and chill. At serving time, pour over ice cubes in puch bowl. Serves 10.

Circa 1970. You can easily multiply the proportions of these ingredients for a larger crowd, as you may with the recipe below.

TRADER VIC PUNCH

24 lemons
24 oranges
6 ounces orgeat syrup
6 ounces sugar syrup

1 1/2 fifths light Puerto Rican rum
1 1/2 fifths dark Jamaican rum

Squeeze juice from lemons and oranges, saving shells. Mix juice with other ingredients. Chill in fridge till party time, then pour into punch bowl filled with ice cubes and cut-up sections of lemon and orange shells. Garnish with mint leaves.
Serves 30.

By Trader Vic.

Coco-Bo

4 ounces unsweetened
pineapple juice
4 ounces Lopez coconut cream
Slice of toasted white bread
Lemon Wheel

Blend juice and coconut cream with two cups crushed ice and pour into coconut mug. Then cut a small square from the piece of toast, douse it in 151 rum, and place it on a lemon wheel floating on top of drink. Ignite bread-cube from safe distance with long-stem match.

As served at Kelbo's restaurant, Los Angeles, California. A family destination since 1947, Kelbo's is now a strip joint called "Fantasy Island."

Tiki Teetotaler

3 ounces unsweetened pineapple juice
3/4 ounce grenadine
1 ounce club soda
Teaspoon heavy cream

Blend juice and grenadine with 3 ounces crushed ice for 10 seconds. Stir in soda. Pour into Collins glass filled with crushed ice. Float cream on top of drink. Garnish with paper parasol stuck into pineapple wedge on rim of glass.

Based on the Princess Anne, from the Hawaiian Punch Pavilion, Sea World, San Diego, California, circa 1960s.

DRINK INDEX

RESOURCE GUIDE

FOR TIKI MUGS:

The mugs shown on our front cover were hand-crafted by Bosko. You can buy them – and many other custom designs – through his mail-order catalogue. Write to P.O. Box 300024, Escondido, CA, 92030, or log on to: www.tikibosko.com.

FOR LIQUORS AND SYRUPS:

The most fully stocked liquor store in the Los Angeles area is Hi-Time Cellars in Costa Mesa; call (714) 650-8463. Beverage Warehouse in West LA, at (310) 306-2822, runs a close second, along with the Vendome chain of stores. In the San Francisco bay area, check your phone book for the local Beverages & More store. Another great Bay Area resource is Donald M. Hughes Distributor, at (650) 967-8258, for everything you need to make tropical drinks *except* the alcohol. Or go straight to the source and visit Trader Vic's Emeryville restaurant, just outside Berkeley at (510) 653-3400, where they sell the complete line of Trader Vic's syrups in the lobby. In Chicago, the biggest and best liquor stores are Zimmerman's, at (312) 332-0012, and Sam's, at (312) 664-4394. Unfortunately, there's no magic phone number for New York, so our best advice is: go out of your neighborhood and scan the shelves of any dusty old liquor store you encounter. We've found interesting ingredients spread all over the city, one and two bottles at a time.

If you live outside a big city, all is not lost. You can **MAIL-ORDER** sugar syrup and a first-rate grenadine from Fee Brothers, which has been in business since 1862. Call (800) 961-3337 (but steer clear of their passion fruit syrup, which, alas, is unsuitable for the type of drinks in this book). For Trader Vic's mixes and syrups, call (800) 200- 5355 to order directly from the Trader's food service division. Energy Beverage Company mail-orders their own brand of orgeat and passion fruit syrup; call (800) 545-1002. Energy will require you to fill a minimum order of a case (about four gallons), but they allow you to mix and match. (Fee Brothers and Trader Vic's mercifully require no minimum.)

FOR FURTHER READING:

Tiki News is the bible of the burgeoning tiki-revival scene. To subscribe to the bi-monthly 'zine, write to 2215-R Market Street #177, San Francisco, CA, 94114. E-mail address: Otto temp@aol.com. Website: http://www.indieweb.com.

FOR THE REAL THING:

There are still a few Polynesian palaces left more or less intact. By far the best drinks and decor can be found at the Mai Kai in Fort Lauderdale, Florida, (305) 563-3272. Trader Vic still maintains outposts in Atlanta, (404) 659-6200; Chicago (312) 917-7317; the San Francisco Bay Area, (510) 653-3400; and Los Angeles, (310) 274-7777. Also in Los Angeles, the Tiki-Ti is a 37-year-old institution that serves authentic drinks in a tiny bar packed with atmosphere and customers; call (213) 669-9381. On the other end of the scale is the massive, eye-popping Kahiki Supper Club in Columbus, Ohio, at (614) 237- 5425. The overall quality of tropical drinks served in Hawaii is suprisingly poor; the only first-rate Mai Tai in the islands can be had at the patio bar of Waikiki's Halekulani Hotel, (808) 923-2311 – a memorable experience as you watch the sun set over the Pacific.

www.ingramcontent.com/pod-product-compliance
Lightning Source LLC
Chambersburg PA
CBHW060132050426
42448CB00010B/2089